1960—1969

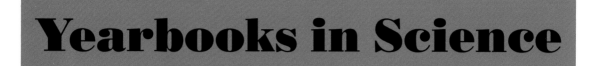

Yearbooks in Science

1960–1969

Tom McGowen

Twenty-First Century Books
A Division of Henry Holt and Company
New York

Twenty-First Century Books
A Division of Henry Holt and Company, Inc.
115 West 18th Street
New York, NY 10011

Henry Holt® and colophon are trademarks of
Henry Holt and Company, Inc.
Publishers since 1866

Published in Canada by Fitzhenry & Whiteside Ltd.
195 Allstate Parkway, Markham, Ontario L3R 4T8

Library of Congress Cataloging-in-Publication Data
Yearbooks in science.
p.   cm.
Includes indexes.
Contents: 1900–1919 / Tom McGowen — 1920–1929 / David E. Newton — 1930–1939 / Nathan Aaseng —
1940–1949 / Nathan Aaseng — 1950–1959 / Mona Kerby — 1960–1969 / Tom McGowen — 1970–1979 / Geraldine
Marshall Gutfreund — 1980–1989 / Robert E. Dunbar — 1990 and beyond / Herma Silverstein.
ISBN 0–8050–3431–5 (v. 1)
1. Science—History—20th century—Juvenile literature. 2. Technology—History—20th century—Juvenile liter-
ature. 3. Inventions—History—20th century—Juvenile literature. 4. Scientists—20th century—Juvenile literature. 5. Engineers—20th century—Juvenile literature. [1. Science—History—20th century. 2.
Technology—History—20th century.]
Q126.4.Y43 1995
609'.04—dc20   95–17485
                                                                                                    CIP
                                                                                                    AC

ISBN 0–8050–3436-6
First Edition 1995
Printed in Mexico
All first editions are printed on acid-free paper ∞.
10 9 8 7 6 5 4 3 2 1

Cover design by James Sinclair
Interior design by Kelly Soong

Cover photo credits
Background: *Vostok 1*, NOVOSTI/Science Photo Library/Photo Researchers, Inc. **Inset images** (clockwise
from top right): *Apollo 11* mission patch, NASA/Airworks/Tom Stack & Associates; chimpanzee © 1979 Tom
McHugh, Photo Researchers, Inc.; Stonehenge © Spencer Grant, Photo Researchers, Inc.; space walk, NASA;
quasar, X-Ray Astronomy Group/Leicester University/SPL/Photo Researchers, Inc.

Photo credits
p. 11: Hughes Research Laboratories/AIP Niels Bohr Library; p. 14: Weber Collection/AIP Niels Bohr Library; p.
16: CERN/Science Photo Library/Photo Researchers, Inc.; p. 20: Jodrell Bank/SPL/Photo Researchers, Inc.; p.
23: John Mead/SPL/Photo Researchers, Inc.; p. 26, 35, 39, 48, 53, 55: UPI/Bettmann; p. 28: Julian Baum/New
Scientist/SPL/Photo Researchers, Inc.; p. 33: Dr. Ken MacDonald/SPL/Photo Researchers, Inc.; p. 37: © Ragnar
Larusson/Photo Researchers, Inc.; p. 40: © Francois Gohier/Photo Researchers, Inc.; p. 44: © C. K.
Lorenz/Photo Researchers, Inc.; p. 49: © Tom McHugh/Photo Researchers, Inc.; p. 51: © 1961 Bob Hines/Used
by permission of Rachel Carson History Project; p. 56: Michael E. DeBakey, M.D./Baylor College of Medicine;
p. 57: ©Hank Morgan/Photo Researchers, Inc.; p. 60: NOVOSTI/SPL/Photo Researchers, Inc.; p. 63:
NASA/TSADO/Tom Stack & Associates; p. 65: USGS/TSADO/Tom Stack & Associates; p. 67, 70: NASA.

For Phil Quinn

Contents

1

PHYSICS

Physics is the science that seeks the causes of natural events and forces—why lightning occurs, what makes the wind blow, what fire is, why things fall down instead of up. The scientists who work in this field are called physicists, but sometimes engineers and scientists from other fields also work in areas of physics. In looking for the causes of things, they often discover new, unsuspected forces, activities, and substances.

At the beginning of the twentieth century, physicists had virtually no understanding of atoms or of the nature of light. But during the first half of the century, a wealth of new knowledge was gathered about the structure and activity of atoms and the form and behavior of light. This knowledge led to several major discoveries and inventions during the decade of the 1960s.

POWER-PACKED LIGHT

Like a number of other major inventions and discoveries of the twentieth century, the invention of the laser was sparked by an idea of the great twentieth-century scientist Albert Einstein.

Einstein's idea concerned light. Light is a form of energy that is produced in tiny "packages" that are called photons. A photon is somewhat like a microscopic hot, glowing spark that travels at incredible speed (186,262 miles, or 299,792 kilometers, per second) and moves in waves, like a ball bouncing along a narrow tunnel. Most sources of light, such as an electric lightbulb or a candle, give off waves of photons in all directions and at different intervals, somewhat like a crowd of people leaving a football stadium—a group of three comes out and heads to the right; seconds later a dozen come out and split up in all directions; moments afterward, five come out and head to the left. But in 1917, Albert Einstein suggested that it might be possible to produce what he called a "coherent" (connected) beam of light in which all the waves would be "in step"; moving regularly one after another in the same direction. Such a beam of light would be very thin, very, very bright, and very, very hot. If it struck something, photons would quickly pile up by the *millions*, creating enough heat to melt their way right through!

It was a long time before Einstein's idea was turned into reality, but the process began in 1954, when physicists built a device that was called a maser. What a maser basically did was *stimulate*, or "excite," atoms, by giving them extra energy.

Everything in the universe—solids, liquids, and gases—is formed of atoms. Most of the time, the atoms in any substance are at their normal level of energy, and they seem to seek to stay that way. If they suddenly *gain* energy, which can happen in a number of ways, they immediately *emit*, or give off, an equal amount of energy in the form of radiation, and get back to their normal state. But when they radiate energy, this can make things happen. The maser invented in 1954 stimulated atoms in a substance such as ammonia gas by sending microwaves (short radio waves) into them. Some of the atoms then released energy in the form of more microwaves, which served to *amplify*, or strengthen, the microwaves sent into them. This was the actual purpose of the maser—to amplify microwaves so that they could better be used for communication. The name *maser* stood for "<u>M</u>icrowave <u>A</u>mplification by <u>S</u>timulated <u>E</u>mission of <u>R</u>adiation."

Physicists quickly saw that what was being done with microwaves could also be done with light. It was known that when atoms were stimulated by receiving energy from photons, they quickly gave off energy in the form of photons. So, the trick was to stimulate a number of atoms into giving off photons all at once. Each of these photons would then cause another atom to become stimulated into giving off a photon, and within a matter of seconds, millions of photons would be produced. If a way of keeping the photons from shooting off in all directions could be found, and if they could be made to all go in one direction, then the thin, powerful beam of light that Einstein had talked about would become possible.

All these problems were solved by 1960. On May 16 of that year, American physicist Theodore Maiman tested the first laser—<u>L</u>ight <u>A</u>mplification by <u>S</u>timulated <u>E</u>mission of <u>R</u>adiation—a device that he had made. For the atoms he needed, he used a 1.6-inch (4-centimeter) rod of artificial ruby,

Theodore Maiman (left) *holds a replica of the first operating laser.*

which, of course, was transparent so light would pass through it. Each end of the rod was coated with metal, which turned the ends into shiny mirrors, facing each other on the inside of the rod. But one end was heavily coated and the other was more thinly coated, so that the rear mirror was "stronger" than the front one.

For his light source, Maiman used a flashlamp—a glass tube filled with gas that acts the same way as a flashbulb for a camera but can be used over many times. The flashlamp was in the form of a coil and was wrapped around the ruby rod.

When Maiman fired an electrical charge into the flashlamp, it flared with an intense burst of light. This instantly stimulated atoms in the ruby rod, which gave off photons. The photons struck the mirrors at the ends of the rod and were reflected off, bouncing back and forth from one mirror to the other at the speed of light. This swift movement of photons back and forth stimulated more atoms to give off photons, building up more and more light within the rod until there was simply too much to hold. Photons began breaking through the weaker mirror at the front of the rod, producing a thin stream of red light that was the world's first laser beam.

Soon, more powerful lasers were being built, firing beams that could instantly melt a hole right through a sheet of steel and even pierce through a diamond, the hardest substance there is! Maiman's ruby laser was what is known as a crystal laser, but other types, such as gas lasers and liquid lasers, were created for different purposes. A ruby laser is a highly efficient drill; a carbon dioxide (gas) laser is used for cutting, welding, and surgery; dye (liquid) lasers are also used for surgery and in scientific research. Einstein's powerful beam of light has become a major tool for the modern world, one that is used in many different ways.

THE WHOLE PICTURE

In science, one discovery or invention often makes another one possible. The invention of the maser made lasers possible, and when lasers appeared, they made it possible for another kind of instrument to be produced.

Some 2,300 years ago, the Greek scientist Aristotle discovered that bright sunlight passing through a tiny hole in the wall of a house caused an upside-down image of what was outside the hole to be cast on the opposite wall inside the house. About 1,800 years later, in Italy, people built special boxes with a tiny hole in one side for casting light images on the other side. And 300 years later, in 1826, French inventor Joseph Niépce found how to preserve such an image by casting it on a sheet of metal coated with chemicals that would turn dark when exposed to light. This was, of course, the beginning of photography (which means "light draw").

For the next 136 years, every photographic picture ever made was always flat, or two-dimensional, showing height and width but no depth. This was because the sunlight or artificial light used to take photographs was formed of only one set of light waves, which could produce only a flat picture. But in 1947, a Hungarian-born British physicist named Dennis Gabor found a way to use light to produce a three-dimensional image.

Dr. Gabor was actually working on a method of improving electron microscopes. An electron microscope uses a beam of electrons to magnify an object and produce an image of it, but Dr. Gabor was experimenting with a way of using a beam of light, instead of electrons, to improve the image. He had found that by using a very powerful light focused through a tiny opening and aimed past an object onto a film, he could get a clear image. But as the light passed the edges of the object he was photographing, it was diffracted, or scattered. When the diffracted light and the rest of the light that had gone past the object without touching it merged on the film, they formed what are known as interference fringes, which were recorded on the film. Gabor realized that because the scattered light had touched the edges of the object being photographed, it contained "information" that could be recorded to show the object in three dimensions.

Gabor saw that the way to do this would be by splitting a beam of light into two parts, so that one would touch the object being photographed and one would not. But the two beams would have to match exactly, and that meant that ordinary light could not be used. Ordinary light is made up of light waves that are going in all directions, so if a beam of ordinary light were split, the two beams made from it would not match. What was needed was what Albert Einstein had called "coherent" light, with all its waves in step, so that the two split beams would match each other exactly. But there was no way to produce such a beam of coherent light in 1947.

Nevertheless, a few scientists and engineers began working with Gabor's idea. Years went by. Then, in 1960, the first laser was tested. It was quickly realized that the coherent beam of light projected by a laser now made Gabor's idea possible. In 1962, Juris Upatnieks and Emmett Leith, two American engineers, put together a device for taking the first three-dimensional photograph. They split a laser beam by sending it through a partly silvered mirror. One beam was focused onto the object being photographed and passed by it onto a glass screen coated with light-sensitive chemicals. The other beam was focused to reflect off a mirror onto the glass screen. Where the two beams merged, interference fringe patterns formed and were recorded on the glass screen. When the screen was developed, it contained an image of the object. At first, Upatnieks and Leith made images of nothing more than printed words, but eventually they produced an image in shades of gray, black, and white of a baby girl standing by a tree.

So, in 1962, three-dimensional photography became possible thanks to the invention of the laser. The kind of three-dimensional picture produced by this method became known as a hologram, meaning "complete record," and the method of making holograms became known as holography.

Besides simply making three-dimensional images, holography has many uses in science and industry. Today, a number of kinds of holograms are made. Some can be looked at in ordinary light and show an object or scene that has length, width, and depth. These are used for such purposes as eye-catching advertisements or for preventing the forgery of credit cards, for a credit card with a hologram on it cannot be counterfeited. Other holograms are looked at with laser light, and these "project" objects and scenes that look completely real—a person can walk all the way around some of them and see them from every side! Holograms are widely used for checking stress—wear and tear—on automobile tires, aircraft wings, jet engines, and other such products. They can be used for making very precise measurements of the velocity of atomic particles. And they can show microscopic objects in amazing detail.

In 1971, Dennis Gabor received the Nobel Prize in physics for the invention of holography.

Dennis Gabor's ideas about using light to produce a three-dimensional image were proposed in 1947 but could not be carried out until 1960.

In the years before the beginning of the twentieth century, most scientists were in agreement that everything in the universe was formed of atoms. They thought of atoms as being the very smallest things there were, somewhat like tiny solid balls that could not be broken up or destroyed in any way.

Then, in 1897, an English physicist known as J. J. Thomson did a very important experiment that wiped out that idea. Thomson's experiment showed that atoms could give off tiny particles (pieces) of themselves that had a negative electrical charge. These particles became known as electrons.

In the first few years of the 1900s, other particles of atoms were found: photons, protons, and neutrons. Photons are particles of light given off by atoms under certain conditions. Protons are particles with a positive electrical charge. Neutrons have no electrical charge. The old idea of atoms as single solid objects was now swept away. The new "picture" of an atom that twentieth-century scientists put together showed that an atom consisted of a nucleus, or center, formed of an equal number of protons and neutrons clustered together, surrounded by a number of electrons whizzing around in orbits. Thus, scientists now thought of atoms as being formed of particles.

At this point, most scientists felt there were probably no other particles in an atom besides electrons, protons, neutrons, and photons. It didn't seem as if any more were really possible. But it is the nature of science and scientists to keep on poking, prying, and digging, to find out more and more about things. And during the first half of the twentieth century, scientists went on to find that there were *lots* of other atomic particles. There are *positrons*, much like electrons but with a positive electrical charge instead of a negative one. *Mesons*, of which there are several types, may be positive, negative, or neutral. *Neutrinos* are formed out of the energy that is produced when a neutron changes into a proton, which happens under certain conditions. By the beginning of the 1960s, more than one hundred new kinds of particles had been discovered. Scientists of the early twentieth century would have been astounded to know that atoms were made up of so many different particles.

However, something even more astounding was yet to come. All these particles were known as "elementary particles," meaning they were as small

Murray Gell-Mann, who discovered quarks along with George Zweig, was awarded the Nobel Prize in physics in 1969.

as possible and there couldn't be anything smaller. But in 1964, two American physicists, Murray Gell-Mann and George Zweig, dropped a bombshell. They announced that two of the major elementary particles, protons and neutrons, were actually formed of *smaller* particles!

Gell-Mann and Zweig believed there were three of these ultratiny particles in all protons and neutrons, and this was why Gell-Mann gave them the strange name *quarks* (pronounced KWORKS). That came from a famous book by an Irish author in which a character speaks of his three children as "the three quarks."

For most physicists in 1964, the idea of quarks was one of the most startling ideas that had been produced in the twentieth century, and they just couldn't believe it at first. But by the end of the 1970s, the existence of quarks had been pretty much proven. Knowledge of quarks has led to new discoveries and new ideas about all the incredible tiny particles that form everything in the universe—including us!

SCIENTIFIC NAMES WITH A TOUCH OF FUN

Most people think that scientists must be rather "stuffy"—sober, serious, and inclined to give long, hard-to-pronounce names to things they discover. But actually, many scientists have a good sense of humor. Like Murray Gell-Mann, who named the new particle he'd helped discover a quark, a lot of scientists have given odd names to things just for fun.

For example, some years after the discovery of the quark, physicists determined that quarks are held together by strange small particles that have a powerful *binding* force. Because these particles literally act like a kind of glue, scientists named them—gluons (glue-ons).

But one of the funniest scientific names ever given to something is found in the field of mathematics. Mathematicians are used to working with large numbers such as million, billion, and trillion, of course, but an American mathematician named Edward Kasner was once working with a number so enormous and little used that it did not have a name—a 1 followed by 100 zeros.

One day, just for fun, he asked his nine-year-old nephew, a boy named Milton Sirotta, what a good name for that number might be. After thinking for a moment, the boy made up a word. Kasner began to use the word as the name for the enormous number, and after a time it became official. And what *is* the official name for a 1 followed by 100 zeros? It's—googol!

2

ASTRONOMY

For the first thirty years of the twentieth century, astronomers still had only optical telescopes—telescopes that are looked through—for studying things in space. Then, in 1931, an American radio engineer named Karl Jansky discovered that outer space seemed filled with radio waves, which could be heard as sounds with the proper equipment. This led to the invention of radio telescopes in the late 1930s—instruments that can be pointed toward any part of space to pick up sounds that might be coming from it. Radio telescopes became a major tool for astronomers in searching out new objects in space, and they were essential to three major astronomical discoveries of the 1960s.

THE QUASI-STELLAR OBJECTS

As the 1960s began, astronomers were fairly certain that most of the major discoveries about space had been made. There probably wasn't anything new to be found, they felt.

In 1960, an American astronomer named Alan Sandage reported that he had found strong radio waves that seemed to be coming from a faint star in a constellation called the Triangle. The star appeared to have a wispy haze of gas around it. Sandage reported that he had made a quick examination of the star's spectrum—the colors of its light—and found it was not like anything he had ever seen before. Most astronomers regarded this as interesting, but it didn't seem to be anything worth getting excited about.

Over the next two years, other astronomers found several similar objects—faint, hazy stars giving off distinct radio waves. Still, no one was much excited. It was generally believed that these stars were probably the remains of supernovas—stars that had exploded.

But a number of astronomers *were* rather curious. American astronomer Maarten Schmidt sat down one day in 1963 to make an examination of the spectrum of one of these hazy radio stars, to see if he could determine exactly what it was. What he found gave him what has been called the shock of his life!

The object, known as 3C-273, had seemed to be just a small, dim, bluish star, not very far away. But it was not a star; it was something completely different, something completely unknown. Rather than being fairly close, it was actually immensely far away, perhaps thousands of millions of light-years. (A light-year is the distance traveled in one year by a beam of light—5.88 trillion miles, or 9.40 trillion kilometers.) This meant that in order for 3C-273 to be visible, it had to be tremendously, titanically bright, brighter than a whole galaxy of *billions* of stars! Yet, compared to a galaxy in size, it was tiny!

This was absolutely fantastic! How could such a small object be so incredibly bright? How could it be so far? What was it? Astronomers were

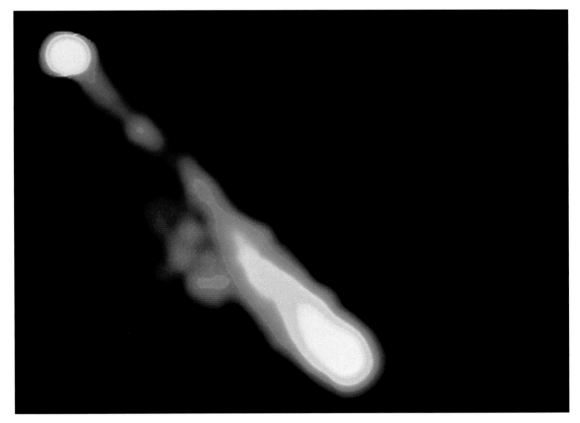

A false-color radio image shows quasar 3C-273, including its enormous jet (bottom right) *and its core* (top left).

certainly excited now, and it was obvious that all the great discoveries had *not* already been made, after all.

3C-273 and the other objects like it were given the name *quasi-stellar objects*, which simply means "starlike" objects. However, that soon got changed into the short name *quasars*. Astronomers began searching for more quasars and searching for the answer to what quasars are. As of the 1990s, more than a thousand quasars had been found, but all the questions about them still weren't answered.

We know that most quasars are about the size of the entire solar system (the sun and nine planets circling it), which is more than 15 billion miles (24 billion kilometers) wide. That seems enormous, but it is infinitesimally tiny compared to an entire galaxy of billions of stars. We know that a quasar can be as much as a trillion times brighter than our sun. We also know that some are more than ten billion light-years from earth, so far that the light we see from them through telescopes was actually given off billions of years ago and has taken that long to reach us now. And they are constantly getting even more distant, moving steadily away from us at tremendous speed.

What we don't know is *how* quasars give off their enormous amounts of energy. What powers them? There are only ideas in answer to those questions. Some scientists think that a quasar may get its power from a gigantic black hole, a collapsed star with such titanic gravity that it can literally suck in anything that is close enough to it. Others disagree. The answer may lie in the future, or it may never be found.

THE PREHISTORIC ASTRONOMERS

Sometimes scientists "cross the line" from their own field of science into another. In the 1960s, an astronomer made a major discovery in the field of archaeology, the science that seeks to learn about the ways of life of people in the past.

On a broad plain in southern England there stands an arrangement of huge rock slabs that is known as Stonehenge, or "stone circle." Actually, it is two and a half circles, one within another. The outer circle is formed of thirty big, rough rectangles of gray rock, about 13 feet (3.9 meters) high, each weighing about 28 tons (25.2 metric tons). Smaller slabs of rock lie across their tops, connecting them. Inside this circle is another ring of smaller stones, and within that is a half circle formed of pairs of 20-foot- (6-meter-) high slabs, with a stone slab lying across the top of each pair. The stones forming the pairs weigh as much as 40 tons (36 metric tons).

Even now, with gasoline-powered cranes and other modern devices, it would be a major project to set these huge stones in their positions. Yet, Stonehenge was actually built *between 3,000 and 4,000 years ago* by prehistoric people who had only such tools as shovels made of the shoulder bones of oxen and pickaxes made of deer antlers! Furthermore, most of the stones came from a rocky area more than 24 miles (38.4 kilometers) away—some even farther—where they were cut and trimmed by hand, using stone wedges and hammers, and then *dragged* all the way to where they were erected, by groups of men hauling them with ropes made of leather.

Many of the stones have fallen down over the centuries, and others were hauled away at times in the distant past, to be used for bridges and buildings. But there are still enough in place to show that erecting Stonehenge had to have been an enormous, gigantic effort that must have taken generations to finish! And the question that scholars and historians and scientists have asked for hundreds of years is, "Why?" *Why* did those prehistoric people spend so much time and effort building this huge arrangement of stone circles? What did it mean to them? What did they use it for? There seemed no way to ever know, for those ancient people did not have any form of writing and left no records of any kind.

One thing is clear, however. Stonehenge had something to do with the *sun.* Some distance beyond the outer ring of stones is a single pair of big stones standing side by side with a narrow space between them, and directly in line with them, a short distance away, is a single, pointed, massive rock. If a person stands inside Stonehenge on the morning of the first day of summer, the longest day of the year, and looks out through the pair of stones at the pointed rock, he or she will see the sun rise directly behind that rock, casting its light between the pair of rocks, into Stonehenge. This could not possibly be an accident. It must have been planned by the builders of Stonehenge.

Trying to find out why Stonehenge was built and what it was used for is really the job of archaeologists, but in the twentieth century, several astronomers became interested in Stonehenge because of its connection with the sun. In 1909, Sir Norman Lockyer, a British astronomer, published a

The sun rises over Stonehenge, an impressive stone circle that scientists believe prehistoric people used as a kind of calendar.

book in which he suggested that Stonehenge was actually a kind of calendar. It could have been used, he said, not only to predict the summer solstice—the longest day of the year, which is the beginning of summer—but also the winter solstice—the shortest day of the year, which marks winter's start.

Lockyer did not have much real proof for this, and most archaeologists and historians paid little attention to his ideas. But in the 1960s, something existed that Lockyer did not have available—computers. And in 1963, an American professor of astronomy, Gerald Hawkins, used a computer to check the connection between the lines extending from the rocks that formed the rings of Stonehenge and the risings and settings of the sun and moon at the time Stonehenge was built. He found that they matched almost perfectly, and the chances of that being an accident were one hundred million to one! Stonehenge apparently *was* a calendar, and also a sort of primitive calculator! It could have been used to precisely show the beginning of each season, to keep track of special days, and even to predict eclipses of the sun and moon.

Several years later, in 1966, another British astronomer, Fred Hoyle, came out in agreement with Hawkins. By means of mathematics, he had determined that the arrangement of the stones could be used to make a number of different kinds of astronomical calculations. This time, archaeologists and historians paid attention to the astronomers, but most did not agree with them. It was preposterous, they felt, to think that primitive people, dressed in animal skins and with nothing but tools made of stone and bone, could have been so clever and knowledgeable. But as time went on, more and more scholars came to agree that Stonehenge must, indeed, have been a kind of gigantic astronomical observatory-calendar-calculator. It had been built by people with a good knowledge of astronomy and mathematics. And this tells us that prehistoric people *were* a good deal more clever and knowledgeable than we might once have thought.

"LONGEST" DAY, "SHORTEST" DAY

A solstice is an event that occurs twice each year, once on about June 21 and the other time on about December 21. The June solstice marks the first day of summer and the December solstice marks the first day of winter. The summer solstice has the longest period of daylight—the longest day—and the winter solstice has the shortest period of sunlight—the shortest day—during the entire year.

Why does this happen? To begin with, you must think of the earth as a ball with an imaginary line running through its middle. That line is earth's axis, around which the whole ball spins. The "top" of the axis is the North Pole and the bottom is the South Pole. But the axis is actually slightly *tilted*, so that part of the time during the year, the North Pole is tilted *toward* the sun and the South Pole is tilted *away* from it, while during the other part of the year, it is just the opposite—the North Pole is tilted away from the sun and the South Pole is tilted toward it.

A solstice occurs during the two times when the earth has reached points, during its year-long orbit around the sun, when the sun is at its greatest distance from the equator, the imaginary line running all the way around earth's exact middle. This means that on that day, sunlight will fall for a longer period of time on the part of earth tilted toward the sun than at any other time, while there will be less sunlight on the part of earth tilted away from the sun. Thus, for the northern part of the earth, the June solstice is the longest day while the December solstice is the shortest, and for the southern part of earth, it is the exact opposite!

Of course, the question of *why* the prehistoric people were so interested in the sun and moon still remains. But many present-day scholars think the answer is simple—religion. They believe that, as well as being a device for keeping track of the movements of the sun and moon, Stonehenge was also a kind of temple at which the sun and moon may have been worshiped as gods. Perhaps. But that is something we may never know, for sure.

LEFTOVERS OF THE BEGINNING

By the middle of the twentieth century, astronomers had worked out two main theories to account for the origin of the universe. One of these was called the steady state theory—the idea that the universe has *always* existed, just about the way it is now. The other theory was called the big bang.

According to the big bang theory, all the matter and energy that now form the universe were once gathered together in a single, incredibly tightly packed, glowing hot mass. There was nothing else, just this fantastically hot fireball surrounded by emptiness. Then, sometime between ten and fifteen billion years ago, the fireball exploded! Fragments of hot, glowing energy went hurtling out in all directions, forming galaxies of stars. This was the beginning of space, time, and the universe.

In 1948, some of the astronomers who had worked out the big bang theory made a prediction. They said that when the early universe cooled down enough for chemical reactions to begin happening, an electromagnetic radiation field was formed. Mathematics showed that this radiation would cool down to a very low temperature, only a few degrees above absolute zero, over twenty billion years, and would remain at the outermost edge of the universe *everywhere* in all directions. Thus, this radiation might someday be located, the scientists predicted, and would be proof that the big bang theory was correct.

In 1965, Arno Penzias and Robert Wilson, two scientists of Bell Laboratories (where research for the American Telephone & Telegraph Company is carried out), were testing a new radio telescope. A radio telescope can pick up sounds given off by objects far, far out in space, of course, but the two men were merely trying to pick up signals from two communications satellites that were orbiting the earth. The signals were quite weak, so Penzias and Wilson had attempted to "tune out" as much background noise as they could. However, they simply couldn't get rid of one particular sound. It was a faint hiss, and no matter where they pointed the telescope, they continued to hear it. It seemed to be coming from *everywhere*. Furthermore, it was the kind of sound that was made by an object with a very low temperature. Checking, the men found that it indicated a temperature only about two degrees above absolute zero.

Penzias and Wilson reported what they had found. Astronomers, astrophysicists, and other scientists were quickly in agreement: what Penzias and Wilson had discovered was the leftover radiation of the big bang, as had been predicted seventeen years before. It was one of the most important discoveries about the universe in history. It was proof that the big bang had truly happened, providing us with positive knowledge of how our universe began.

Arno Penzias (left) *and Robert Wilson stand in front of the device they used to discover radiation left over from the beginning of the universe—the big bang.*

MYSTERIOUS RADIO WAVES FROM SPACE

On an August day in 1967, a young Englishwoman found what some scientists actually thought might be a *message* from far out in space!

Jocelyn Bell was an astronomy student at Cambridge University in England. She had been assigned to study charts of the radio waves that were picked up from space by the university's radio telescope. One day as she was examining the charts, which were produced daily, she noticed that some radio waves that had been picked up at about midnight of the day before had apparently been "blinking" on and off very rapidly.

Some radio waves from space do seem to waver, or go on and off, much as the light of stars seems to twinkle. What causes this is that the waves pass by the sun and run into what is known as the "solar wind"—streams of atomic particles given off by the sun and flying through space. When radio waves bump into particles, it makes their sound waver on a radio telescope. Jocelyn Bell knew this, of course, but she realized that at midnight the whole width of the earth would have been between the sun and the incoming radio waves. So, it couldn't have been the solar wind making the radio waves waver off and on, for that would have been blocked by the earth.

Bell checked to see if some other form of interference such as a thunderstorm or surge of electrical power had taken place at the time the radio waves were picked up. This could have been responsible for the blinking of the waves. But no such thing had happened.

When Bell reported her findings, a few astronomers thought—perhaps only half seriously—that maybe the blinking was *deliberate*, and the radio signals were nothing less than a *message* from somewhere in space! Some scientists jokingly named the blinking radio waves LGMs, standing for "little green men."

However, it quickly became obvious that the wavering waves really did not make any sense as a message. They formed a steady, regular "pulse" that was obviously not a code or mathematical sequence. Furthermore, the record of the waves showed that whatever was producing them was moving the same way that stars move. So, the waves couldn't be coming from a planet, where intelligent creatures might be living. Astronomers decided that Jocelyn Bell had discovered a new kind of space object—a radio star that *pulsed*, giving off steady, rhythmic bursts of radio waves. They named it a pulsar.

But what would cause a star to pulse in such a way? In the years following Jocelyn Bell's discovery, we have found out. A pulsar is the remains of a star that has exploded!

Stars "die," or come to an end, just like everything else. But they do it in different ways, depending on the kind of star they are. Stars that are many times bigger than our sun first explode, becoming what are called supernovas. In some cases, the core, or very center of the star, collapses in the explosion, and the star's enormous gravity pulls the collapsed material into an incredibly tightly packed mass. The protons and electrons of the atoms making up the mass form into neutrons, which have no electrical charge. The remains of the collapsed core become an object that is no more than a dozen or so miles wide but has as much mass, or substance, as our sun, so tightly squeezed together that a 1-inch (2.5-centimeter) cube of it would weigh mil-

An artist's concept of a pulsar—a neutron star that is a source of regularly pulsing radio waves.

lions of tons! This object is called a neutron star, the smallest kind of star there is.

Neutron stars give off radio waves that travel in only one direction, along the star's magnetic pole. Therefore, as the star rotates, or turns, the beam of radio waves sweeps around in a circle. Every time the star's magnetic pole turns to face the earth, the beam of radio waves comes speeding toward us and can be picked up as a "burst" by radio telescopes. As the magnetic pole turns away, the beam sweeps on and is lost to us, causing the radio telescope to indicate that the radio waves have switched off. This is what causes the on and off pulse. Neutron stars rotate very rapidly, and the period between their pulses may be from only one-thousandth of a second to about four seconds.

Since Jocelyn Bell discovered the first pulsar, or neutron star, in 1967, more than 400 others have been found.

3

GEOLOGY

Geology is the science that studies the activities and history of earth. In the first half of the twentieth century, more and more geologists began studying the forces that change the earth, such as volcanoes and earthquakes. Some began to investigate the sea as a source of information.

In the branch of geology called paleontology, the study of prehistoric life, dinosaurs were a major interest, and museums scrambled to put together dinosaur skeletons for people to see. There were important discoveries made about dinosaurs, such as that they had scaly skin, like modern reptiles, and that they hatched from eggs, as modern reptiles do. Thus, it was generally believed that dinosaurs must have been much like the reptiles of today—cold-blooded, slow moving, and not very intelligent. For a number of paleontologists, the origin of human beings was a major interest, and tremendous advances in knowledge about this subject were made in the first half of the century.

Very early in the century, the German scientist Alfred Wegener presented the theory that the world's continents had once been joined together in a single gigantic "supercontinent," which he called Pangaea, meaning "all the land." Some tremendous force had broken the single continent into the seven continents of today, Wegener insisted. Most scientists thought Wegener's ideas were ridiculous, but a few grew interested in them, and this led to a revolutionary discovery about the structure of the earth, in the 1960s.

THE MOVING CONTINENTS

For about the first forty years of the twentieth century, geologists and other scientists generally thought of the earth as being somewhat like a baked apple that had been taken out of the oven and put on a windowsill to cool.

They believed the earth had been formed out of hot molten material that had gradually cooled as the heat leaked away into the cold of space. As the outside of the earth grew cool, it had wrinkled like the skin of a baked apple, scientists thought, forming mountains and valleys. And, like the skin of an apple, earth's "skin"—the layer of rock covering the entire globe and forming the earth's surface—was rigid and unmoving, according to geologists.

In 1912, Alfred Wegener had challenged this idea. The earth's surface was *not* rigid and unable to move, Wegener insisted; it moved! He presented evidence showing that all of the part of earth's surface that was above the ocean had once been joined together, forming a single gigantic supercontinent. But this huge landmass had broken up, said Wegener, and the pieces of it had *moved*, drifting apart to form the continents as they are today.

Almost all other scientists heaped scorn on Wegener's ideas. How could the continents move through the solid rock of the rest of the surface? they questioned. Some of them believed Wegener was a hoaxer; others thought he was simply foolish. Wegener died in 1930, and as time passed, all but a few scientists forgot about what he had called his drifting continents theory.

During World War II, 1939 to 1945, there was a great spurt in technology, with many new instruments and methods of doing things put into use. In the late 1940s, scientists began to study the ocean floor using radar, sonar, and other new devices produced during the war. They began to discover startling, unsuspected things!

Geologists had always believed that the part of earth's surface under the sea, which had never been worn away by erosion as the part in air had, was the oldest rock on the planet, billions of years old. They also believed that sediment, the material dumped into the sea by rivers, had been building up on the sea bottom for billions of years and was probably a good 12 miles (19.2 kilometers) thick. But now that they were able to actually measure the sediment, they were astounded to find that it was less than a mile thick. Why should this be? They were even more astounded to discover that the rock beneath the sediment was *not* billions of years old but was actually fairly new! How could that be possible?

More discoveries followed. In 1953, it was found that there was literally an enormous *crack* running along the sea bottom beneath the Atlantic Ocean, from which heat was rising. Then it was discovered that this crack was actually in the middle of an awesome 40,000-mile- (64,000-kilometer-)

long mountain range that runs along beneath the world's oceans, forming a curving chain that spans the entire planet!

In 1960, geologist Harry Hess, who had been studying the ocean floor for years, put some of these facts together and came up with an astonishing new version of an old idea. He suggested that the ocean floors were *moving* and carrying the world's continents along with them! This was Alfred Wegener's continental drift theory of forty-eight years before, but Hess, unlike Wegener, had been able to find out how it was happening. He explained that molten rock was constantly seeping up through the crack in the ocean floor and spreading outward to harden and form a *new* floor at a rate of about one-half inch (1.25 centimeters) a year. This explained the heat that was coming up from the crack; it was the heat of the molten rock seeping up. It also explained why the ocean floor wasn't billions of years old—it was being completely replaced over every few hundred million years. And it explained why sediment didn't build up on the ocean floor—it was being absorbed by the hot rock constantly oozing up.

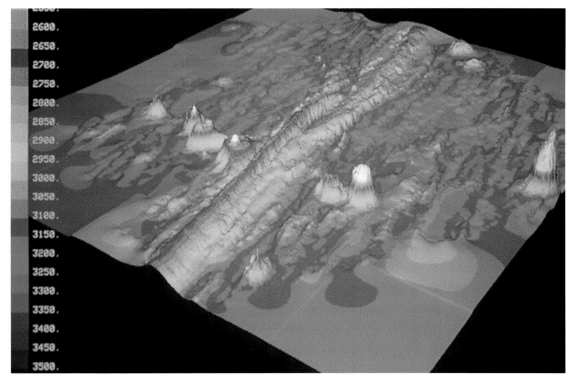

A false-color, three-dimensional map of part of the East Pacific rise, a mid-ocean ridge lying to the west of Central America. The ridge marks the boundary between two tectonic plates where molten rock rises to the surface, forming new sea floor.

Hess suggested that even as the new sea floor was being formed, the old floor was being sucked down into the deep trenches that lie along the edges of the continents. It was this rise and fall of molten hot and solid cold rock that caused the continents to move, Hess explained.

Most scientists of the 1960s didn't like Hess's theory any more than those of 1912 had liked Wegener's. But a few began researching along the lines Hess had presented, and evidence for "sea floor spreading," as it was called, and for continental drift began to grow. In 1967, geologist Tuzo Wilson suggested that undersea trenches, ridges, and mountain ranges were actually the edges of vast curved "plates" of rock that formed the entire crust of the earth and were in constant motion. Geophysicist Jason Morgan showed how such plates could move across the curved surface of the earth. Within a year, a group of seismologists (earthquake researchers) announced that evidence from earthquake activity around the world proved that Morgan was right.

Thus, the sixty-year-old idea of the earth as a cooling, shrinking ball covered with a rigid shell of rock was swept away. Now we know that earth's crust is actually formed of six gigantic sections of rock and about a dozen smaller ones, some 60 miles (96 kilometers) thick, that are sliding very slowly over the hot molten rock beneath them, carrying the continents. Harry Hess's announcement in 1960 proved that Alfred Wegener had essentially been right and set the stage for the new science called plate tectonics, which has given us a better understanding of the workings of the earth.

THE FIRST HUMANS

Two million years ago, Africa was swarming with many more kinds of animals than it has today. In addition to lions and leopards, there were tiger-size saber-toothed cats with 6-inch- (15-centimeter-) long fangs. There were several different kinds of elephantlike animals. And while Africa now has only two kinds of apes—gorillas and chimpanzees—there were a number of different kinds of apelike creatures roaming the African plains and woodlands of two million years ago.

Some of these were four-footed animals, as gorillas and chimpanzees are. They walked bent over, using their hands as well as their feet. But some of the others walked upright on two legs, as humans do. Paleontologists have found a number of skulls and bones of these upright-walking apelike creatures. One kind was about 4 feet (1.2 meters) tall and slimly built. They have been named *Australopithecus afarensis*, or "southern ape of the Afar region (of Africa)." Another kind was larger—about 5 feet (1.5 meters) tall—and heavily built, like a gorilla. These are known as *Australopithecus robustus*, meaning "sturdy southern ape."

But although the names of these two creatures mean "ape," they were not really apes. Apes cannot stand, walk, or run upright on two legs as these creatures could. And from the size of the skulls of these creatures, paleontologists judge that they were a little smarter than gorillas, chimpanzees, or other kinds of apes. So, they are called hominids, which means "humanlike." They were not true humans, but they were part of the human "family."

In 1960, paleontologists Louis and Mary Leakey, of Kenya, in eastern Africa, were searching for fossils at the site of an ancient lake in Tanzania, a country next to Kenya. One of their young sons, Jonathan, was with them, and one day he found part of the fossil skull of what looked like a very young *Australopithecus afarensis*. Later, near where the skull was found, the Leakeys also found the child's leg bones, hand bones, and the bones of one foot. It quickly became clear that the kind of creature the child was had a bigger brain than either *Australopithecus afarensis* or *robustus* and bones that were more like those of a human than the bones of either of those two creatures.

Mary (foreground) *and Louis Leakey are shown digging for evidence of prehistoric man. The Leakeys made major contributions to the search for our first human ancestor.*

The Leakeys were famous paleontologists. Louis had made the major discovery that Africa was the place where human beings had begun, and Mary had also made a number of highly important discoveries. They decided that what they and Jonathan had found was nothing less than the remains of one of the first true human beings! The Leakeys named it *Homo habilis*, meaning "skillful human," because they felt sure that its kind had probably been the first human ancestor that could *make* things.

Not all scientists of that time were willing to agree that the Leakeys had found the first human. Many thought that *Homo habilis* was probably just an *Australopithecus afarensis*. But as time went on, there were more and more discoveries of *Homo habilis*—a nearly complete adult skull, bones, remains of campsites, and pieces of stone that had been deliberately chipped to be used as cutting blades. Most scientists finally agreed that *Homo habilis* was, indeed, the first kind of human, which had evolved from the hominid *Australopithecus afarensis*.

Today, a great deal is known about *Homo habilis*. They were probably slim, dark-skinned, shaggy-haired people, with faces that would seem rather apelike to us. They lived in groups of as many as twenty, moving about the edges of lakes and streams, where they made camps for short periods of time. They may have been able to build crude huts, but they did not know how to make fire. However, they could chip sharp flakes off stones and use the flakes to cut up the animals they ate. They had the beginning of human intelligence. The Leakeys' discovery had led us to our first human ancestor.

A GLIMPSE OF THE CHANGING WORLD

On the morning of November 14 in 1963, the crew of an Icelandic fishing boat in the Atlantic Ocean stared in awe at an astonishing sight. Billows of thick black smoke were pouring up out of a spot in the water!

The fishing boat turned back toward Iceland, 22 miles (35.2 kilometers) away, and notified authorities of what was happening. Icelandic geologists were quickly alerted, and many were soon heading out in boats toward the place from which the smoke was rising. They knew what was happening; an underwater volcano was erupting!

All through the day, geologists watched as smoke continued to roll up from the surface of the sea, accompanied by a deep rumbling noise. Near nightfall, it could be seen that a ridge of ash and rock was building up in the water. The underwater volcano was pouring forth tons of hot ash and molten lava, which quickly hardened in the cool water, piling up in an ever-higher mound that would eventually rise above the water's surface. The geologists were thrilled to realize that they could be watching the formation of a new island if the mound was not destroyed by waves when it began to reach above the water.

When the sun rose the next morning, the mound could clearly be seen: a dull black lump formed of ash and cinders, thrusting up above the waves. Over it boiled a rolling cloud of smoke, thousands of feet high, out of which rained ash and "bombs" of lava. As time went on, it became obvious that the mound was not going to be washed away and that it was growing. A new island had been born!

Iceland was settled by Norse Vikings some 1,100 years ago and has strong Norse traditions. And so, the Icelanders named the new little island and the volcano that was forming it Surtsey, after a character from ancient

To the amazement of fishermen and scientists alike, an underwater volcano erupted and created a new island, called Surtsey, off the coast of Iceland.

Norse mythology—Surt, the king of the Fire Giants, who ruled a land of rock and flame.

Surtsey continued to erupt off and on until 1967. By that time, the island was more than a mile wide and 380 feet (116 meters) above the water at its highest point. Iceland, too, was formed by volcanic eruptions that began some twenty million years ago. Iceland is still growing, at the rate of about an inch a year, as a result of the constant upflow of molten rock from the sea floor below it. Iceland and Surtsey are both actually tips of volcanic mountains that are part of the 12,000-mile- (19,200-kilometer-) long mountain range running along beneath the Atlantic Ocean.

The birth of Surtsey in 1963 was a major event for geologists. For the first time in history, they had the opportunity to actually see how the titanic forces of the earth create islands as new parts of the ever-changing face of the world.

A New Kind of Dinosaur

It was in the 1820s that scientists first discovered there had once been enormous reptiles living on the earth millions of years ago. The reptiles were given the name *dinosaurs* in 1842. For more than 120 years after that, most scientists thought that dinosaurs must have been much like the reptiles of today—clumsy, slow-moving creatures with sprawled-out legs, dragging their tails on the ground behind them.

In 1964, something happened that would change that picture of dinosaurs forever.

On an August day in that year, paleontologists John Ostrom and Grant Meyer were walking down the slope of a dome-shaped hill in Montana. Suddenly, they both saw something that started them rushing down the hill as fast as they could go. What they saw were the skeleton fingers of a large clawed hand sticking up out of a patch of rock!

The two men cleared away as much rock as they could with their bare hands and uncovered what was clearly the three-fingered, sharp-clawed front foot of a small dinosaur. The next day, they returned and, after some chipping and digging with tools, uncovered a rear foot. They stared at it in amazement, because it was not like any dinosaur foot they had ever seen. Instead of having three similar toes with short, pointed claws, this foot's first, or inner, toe bore a long, wicked-looking curved claw that was shaped like the old-fashioned grain-cutting tool called a sickle. Ostrom and Meyer knew they had found a brand-new kind of dinosaur!

Over a period of two years, they found enough bones to make up nearly complete skeletons of three of the new dinosaurs. The creatures were small: no more than 13 feet (3.9 meters) long from tip of nose to end of tail and only about 5 feet (1.5 meters) high. But they looked like tiny *Tyrannosauruses!* Their sharp teeth showed they were meat-eaters, and their sharp claws showed they were probably predators—animals that hunted and attacked prey. And they definitely were a new kind of dinosaur—a startlingly different creature that was going to change everyone's idea of what all dinosaurs must have been like.

For, when John Ostrom studied the new dinosaurs' bones, he discovered some remarkable things. The creatures' tails were not flexible and snaky, like the tail of a lizard. The bones of the tail were locked together in a way that meant the tail must have always been stiff and straight. Ostrom also found that the "wrist" and "hand" bones of the little dinosaurs' front feet fit together in a way that showed the creatures were able to twist and turn their "hands" much the same way that humans can. And the way the bones of the legs and feet fit together showed that the little dinosaurs must have used that big sickle-shaped claw on each first toe as a vicious, slashing weapon!

What did this mean? It meant that these dinosaurs

John Ostrom holds a dinosaur claw—the clue that led to his discovery of a new species of dinosaur.

39

had been very fast-moving, agile, and deadly creatures! They ran on two legs with their tails extended straight out for balance, enabling them to make sudden twists and turns as they chased prey. They could grab prey with their "hands" and hold it, while they lashed out with a vicious kick from one of those big, curved toe claws that would rip the prey open with a killing wound!

Because of that deadly curved claw on each foot, Ostrom named the new dinosaur *Deinonychus*, which means "terrible claw." *Deinonychus* was a far cry from the idea of slow-moving, tail-dragging dinosaurs that paleontologists had held for almost a century and a half. Its discovery made paleontologists begin to rethink and restudy the movement and agility of all dinosaurs. Our picture of dinosaurs today, as fast-moving animals that walked with straight legs and extended tails, had its beginning with the discovery of *Deinonychus*.

This life-sized, animated model shows Deinonychus, *a meat-eating predator, standing over its prey.*

IS THAT "TERRIBLE CLAW'S" COUSIN IN YOUR BACKYARD?

Scientists have known for a long time that birds are descended from reptiles. Many parts of a bird's body are much like parts of a reptile's body. A bird's feathers are made of the same substance (called keratin) as a reptile's scales and are actually a kind of stretched-out scale, split into many branches. The feet of most birds are scaly and clawed, like many kinds of reptile feet. And birds hatch out of hard-shelled eggs just as reptiles do. But the question for scientists was, What *kind* of reptile were birds descended from?

That question seemed to have been answered when *Deinonychus*—"terrible claw"—was discovered. After he'd had a good length of time to learn all he could about *Deinonychus*, Dr. John Ostrom decided that *Deinonychus* had a lot more in common with birds—like the fast-moving roadrunner and the hard-kicking ostrich—than it did with a sluggish slow-moving turtle or alligator. He suggested that very possibly, both birds and *Deinonychus*, as well as dinosaurs like it, were all descended from a common ancestor. In other words, the kind of reptile that was the ancestor of birds was a *dinosaur*!

Most paleontologists now think that is probably right. So, when you see a robin rushing across your backyard to catch a bug, you're probably looking at *Deinonychus*'s cousin!

A Discovery in Antarctica

The continents of Africa and Antarctica are as different from each other as any two places could possibly be. Africa is a warm land of deserts, expanses of thick forest, long rivers, and great lakes, and it is home to many kinds of animals. Most of Antarctica is a frozen desolation of ice and snow that is the coldest part of the world. Nothing lives in these vast snowy regions beyond the coasts.

Despite their great differences today, the German scientist Alfred Wegener had insisted, in 1912, that Africa and Antarctica had once been joined together, millions of years ago, with all the other continents. By the 1960s, most scientists had decided that Wegener had been right. The new science of plate tectonics showed how Africa and Antarctica could have been split apart from each other. But there was no actual *proof* that they had ever been joined.

Beneath Antarctica's ice and snow there is rock, and along the coasts and in some other places, the rock lies uncovered. Since the late 1950s, paleontologists had been visiting Antarctica to dig in the rocky areas in search of fossils that might reveal what the continent had been like before it became covered with ice, some thirty million years ago. Fossils of many plants and animals that had been found up to 1969 clearly showed that Antarctica was once a warm place, with forests. But this was still no actual proof that it had ever been joined to any other continent.

In 1969, American paleontologists Edwin Colbert and David Elliot were searching for fossils in Antarctica. They were rather hoping to find the bones of a dinosaur, for no dinosaur fossils had ever been discovered in Antarctica up to that time. If a dinosaur were found, it might well be a new kind of dinosaur.

The two men did find something, but it was not a dinosaur and it certainly was not anything new. It was the skull and some of the bones of a small creature that paleontologists already knew a lot about—a four-legged reptile about the size of a large dog that had lived some 200 million years ago. It had been named *Lystrosaurus*.

This find didn't seem to be anything worth getting very excited about, but Colbert and Elliot *were* excited. For they realized that what they had found was the proof that Alfred Wegener had been right. There was now no doubt that Africa and Antarctica had, indeed, once been joined together!

The reason Colbert and Elliot knew this was because fossil bones of exactly the same creature they had just dug up had also been discovered in Africa, many years before. Clearly, *Lystrosaurus* had once lived in what is now Africa as well as in Antarctica. But there was no way that a *Lystrosaurus* could have gotten from Africa *to* Antarctica across 2,000 miles (3,200 kilometers) of ocean and no way that *Lystrosaurus*es could have developed in exactly the same way in two different places. Finding *Lystrosaurus* fossils in both Africa and Antarctica could only mean that when these animals had been alive, some 200 million years ago, Africa and Antarctica had been part of a single piece of land where many *Lystrosaurus*es had lived. Millions of years after the two animals had died and been fossilized, the piece of land had broken apart, leaving one *Lystrosaurus* fossil on one new continent and the other fossil on another continent.

Today, we know that Africa, Antarctica, and all the other continents were once joined together in the single gigantic supercontinent that Alfred Wegener called Pangaea. Scientists hailed the 1969 discovery of *Lystrosaurus* in Antarctica as one of the final pieces of evidence that showed this to be true. As fossils go, it was rather commonplace, but as a piece of information about the way the world changes, the discovery of *Lystrosaurus* in Antarctica was a major find.

A DIFFERENT IDEA ABOUT DINOSAURS

The animals that we call reptiles—alligators, crocodiles, lizards, snakes, turtles, and tuataras—all have certain things in common. They all have scaly skin. Nearly all of them hatch out of hard-shelled eggs that are always laid on land, never in water as fish and frog eggs are. They are all "cold-blooded." These are the things that *make* them reptiles.

When we say that reptiles are cold-blooded, we mean that their bodies have no way of heating themselves, as ours do. We belong to the group of creatures called mammals, which are all "warm-blooded," with bodies that are always warm inside, no matter whether the air around them is hot or cold. Birds are like this, too. But a reptile's body is affected by the temperature of the air. In hot weather, reptiles are active and able to move about quickly and do things. But in cool weather, reptiles generally become slow moving and listless, and in very cold weather they cannot move at all. Their heartbeats slow down, and they are just barely alive.

When fossil skeletons of dinosaurs began to be discovered, more than 150 years ago, scientists quickly recognized that these creatures had been reptiles. And, of course, from then on most scientists automatically believed that dinosaurs, like present-day reptiles, must have had scaly skin, must have hatched from eggs, and must have been cold-blooded. A dinosaur skeleton with fossilized skin on it, discovered in 1908, proved that dinosaurs did have scaly skin. Fossilized dinosaur eggs, discovered in 1923, proved that dinosaurs did hatch from eggs. With this evidence showing that dinosaurs were just like modern-day reptiles, paleontologists were quite certain that they had been cold-blooded as well.

And so, the picture of dinosaurs that was built up over a good hundred years was of creatures that acted very much like a lizard or crocodile. Dinosaurs probably moved quite slowly, dragging their tails along on the ground, said paleontologists. They probably spent long periods basking in bright sunshine, storing up enough heat in their bodies so that they could move about and search for food. If they got too warm from long periods in hot sunshine, they probably immersed themselves in the water of a lake or river to cool down, as many present-day reptiles do. After all, dinosaurs were reptiles, and this is how reptiles behave.

In the year 1969, the first nationwide convention of North American paleontologists was held in the Field Museum of Natural History, in Chicago. There were many speakers giving talks on things of interest to paleontologists. One of the

Snakes, and other cold-blooded reptiles, bask in the sun to raise their body temperature.

speakers was Dr. John Ostrom, who had discovered the new dinosaur *Deinonychus* in 1964. During his talk, Ostrom presented an astounding new idea. He suggested that dinosaurs might have been *warm*-blooded. In other words, Ostrom was saying that, in one way, a dinosaur might have been more like a wolf or an ostrich than like a lizard or an alligator!

Like most theories proposed by scientists, Ostrom's idea was based on strong evidence and sound reasoning. He pointed out that, as is obvious from their skeletons, dinosaurs stood and walked upright, with their legs straight beneath them. Modern, cold-blooded reptiles don't walk this way; their legs are sprawled out at the sides, so that they are generally *crawling* when they move, with their bellies and tails dragging on the ground. The only animals that stand and walk upright today are the warm-blooded ones: mammals (dogs, cats, horses, humans, et cetera) and birds. Ostrom suggested that only warm-blooded creatures *could* walk this way, because only the "heating system" of warm-blooded animals provides sufficient energy. He also pointed out that the body shapes of many dinosaurs show clearly that they must have been agile and fast moving, in a way that no present-day reptile could possibly be.

Many paleontologists simply could not accept Ostrom's idea of warm-blooded reptiles. Others hailed it as a sensational concept that helped explain a lot of puzzling things about dinosaurs. To this day, the matter is still not settled among paleontologists, and there are bits of evidence that support both sides. Some paleontologists believe that all dinosaurs were, indeed, warm-blooded, while others think they were all cold-blooded. Some believe that not all dinosaurs were the same, that some of them were warm-blooded and others cold-blooded. And there are a few paleontologists who think that dinosaurs actually may not have been either entirely warm-blooded *or* cold-blooded but may have had some "middle" way that enabled them to do things modern reptiles cannot do. Thus, Dr. Ostrom's theory certainly caused paleontologists to begin looking at dinosaurs in a new way. Whether they think that dinosaurs were warm-blooded or not, all paleontologists now agree that these creatures were very different from any kind of reptile living today and that there is really nothing exactly like them now on earth. They may well have been the "highest" form of reptile possible, and the reptiles of today may be nothing more than "leftovers."

4

BIOLOGY

Biology is the science that studies life—the relationships, activities, disorders, and life processes of living things. Biology developed a number of new branches and new methods during the first half of the twentieth century. Genetics, the study of how living things pass their characteristics along from generation to generation, began to develop in the very first years of the century, as did ecology, the study of the relationships of living things to each other and to their environment. In the 1930s, the science of ethology, the study of animal behavior, had its beginning. By the middle of the century, these new branch sciences were becoming very important.

Twentieth-century biologists made more and more use of technology and mathematics in their work. Medicine, a major branch of biology, gained tremendously from the twentieth-century expansion of technology in the Western world.

A STUDY OF OUR CLOSEST RELATIVES

In June of the year 1960, a young Englishwoman began the longest study of a wild animal species that has ever been made. Twenty-six-year-old Jane Goodall went into a wild part of the African country of Tanzania and began to carefully watch and keep a record of the way of life of a small group of chimpanzees.

Chimpanzees are members of the ape family, which also includes gorillas, orangutans, and gibbons, and are the most closely related animals to humans. A chimpanzee is from $3\frac{1}{4}$ to $5\frac{1}{2}$ feet (about 1 to 1.65 meters) high, and weighs from 90 to 110 pounds (40.5 to 49.5 kilograms). They are actually four-footed animals that walk and run bent over, using their hands as well as

Jane Goodall has made the study of chimpanzees her life's work.

their feet. However, they are also able to use their hands much as humans do, for holding and handling things. They live in forested parts of central Africa, in small groups that wander about over an area of 10 to 20 miles (16 to 32 kilometers) in search of food—mainly fruits, seeds, and leaves. Chimpanzees live from forty to sixty years in zoos and about thirty to thirty-eight years in the wild.

Jane Goodall located a small band of chimpanzees that lived in a forest on a mountainside. It was nearly a year before they grew sufficiently used to seeing her so that she could get fairly close to them. But then, she was able to watch them every day, from dawn to dusk, at very close range. In time, she learned things about chimpanzees that had never even been suspected.

Scientists had believed that chimpanzees ate nothing but vegetable foods, such as fruits and leaves. But Jane Goodall discovered that they also eat meat, of such animals as monkeys, baboons, and wild pigs, which they hunt and kill. She also found that chimpanzees sometimes actually make and use *tools*, such as bits of twig and vine with which they dislodge termites from their nests in order to eat them.

They also wad leaves into clumps that they use like sponges, to sop up puddles of rainwater to drink. All of this was astounding information, because it had been believed that only humans could figure out how to make tools for special purposes.

What was perhaps even more astounding was that Goodall saw that chimpanzees actually fight wars and kill one another! She saw one band of chimps deliberately wipe out another over a period of time, for no reason at all as far as she could tell.

Jane Goodall studied chimpanzees off and on for more than thirty years, often living right among them for years at a time. Her study was of great importance, because it revealed that chimpanzees are exceptionally intelligent and very humanlike and are probably very much like our early apelike ancestors were. Their way of life can show us much about how our early ancestors probably lived. Goodall's studies also helped bring attention to problems that humans are causing for chimpanzees. These creatures, our closest animal relatives, are becoming more and more endangered by the cutting of their forests and damage to their environment. Where there were once about 10,000 chimpanzees in the part of Africa where Jane Goodall began studying them, there are now probably no more than 2,500.

A chimpanzee chews on a twig to turn it into a tool for catching termites.

WHAT'S THE DIFFERENCE BETWEEN APES AND MONKEYS?

Scientists call chimpanzees apes, but many people who don't know any better call them monkeys. What is the difference between apes and monkeys?

There are four main kinds of apes—chimpanzees, gorillas, orangutans, and gibbons. Apes are large animals—a gorilla standing upright may be as much as 6 feet (1.8 meters) tall—whereas most monkeys are quite small. No apes have tails, while most kinds of monkeys have tails. Apes have longer fingers and toes than monkeys.

But the biggest difference is that apes are more intelligent than monkeys and are much more like humans. Apes resemble humans more closely and are more closely related to humans than any other kind of animal. For example, there are many differences between human blood and the blood of, say, a horse, but there are almost no differences between human blood and chimpanzee blood. Scientists feel there is strong evidence that apes and humans are both descended from one kind of creature that lived millions of years ago. But monkeys do not share that ancestor.

A WARNING TO THE WORLD

In 1962, a book was published that quite literally turned the world in a different direction. It caused millions of people to make up their minds to do something about a serious danger that threatened them, which they hadn't even been aware of before.

The book's author, Rachel Carson, was a marine biologist—a scientist who studies the life of the ocean. But the book was not about the ocean. Entitled *Silent Spring*, it was a warning about the danger that threatened the world from the use of chemical pesticides and herbicides—poisonous substances that were sprayed on farm fields, orchards, and gardens to kill unwanted insects and weeds.

The use of chemical pesticides and herbicides had become widespread in the late 1940s. One pesticide that was considered especially useful was known as DDT. During World War II, it was widely used to protect American soldiers on South Pacific islands from catching malaria, which is spread by mosquitoes. DDT was heavily sprayed in tents and barracks where soldiers lived and slept, and it proved effective. Later, after the war, DDT was used to control insects on farmlands and in forests. It was generally sprayed from airplanes flying low over an area and releasing clouds of DDT in the form of a wet mist that drifted down and covered plants with a protective coating. Much of it also soaked into the ground.

By the late 1950s, a number of scientists and other people had become aware that DDT and other chemical poisons weren't killing only insects, they were killing many other things as well. In areas that had been sprayed with DDT, songbirds, such as robins, were found dead by the hundreds. Investigating why this had happened, scientists found that earthworms, which robins eat, had become poisoned with DDT that had entered their bodies, and the birds were dying from eating the poisonous worms. Useful creatures of the soil, which help plants grow, had been affected, too. It was also found that DDT in the soil was being carried into ponds and streams by rainwater and was poisoning fish, frogs, and other creatures.

Rachel Carson, scientist and author, in a photograph taken in 1961.

People were found to be in danger from pesticides and herbicides as well. In 1959, it was discovered that a herbicide called aminotriazole could cause cancer, and this herbicide was on and in fruits and vegetables that people ate.

In her book *Silent Spring*, Rachel Carson presented information about all the dangers to animals, plants, and people from the widespread use of chemical poisons such as DDT and aminotriazole. She described how soil and water were being polluted and how plants and wildlife were being destroyed. She pointed out that more and more chemicals were flooding into the world we all live in and affecting the food chain that all creatures, including humans, depend on for life. She showed that almost no thought was being given to the possible harmful effects these substances might have. The title of her book, *Silent Spring*, was actually a warning that someday the springtime, which has always been ushered in by the cheery sound of bird-songs after a gloomy winter, might be *silent*, because all the songbirds would be dead—killed by chemical pollution.

Rachel Carson had not made a major discovery, such as finding a new object in space, or presented a new theory, such as Einstein's theory of relativity, but her book was of *major* importance. It alerted people to the danger of pollution, and because of it, many changes, such as the banning of DDT, were eventually made. *Silent Spring* was the actual beginning of the environmental movement.

A Change of Heart

The heart is a hollow muscle about the size of a fist that is actually a pump, pumping blood through the veins and arteries to all parts of the body. If something should happen to that muscle so that it cannot keep on pumping, the body it is in would quickly die. Unfortunately, a lot of things can happen to make the heart stop pumping. In the United States alone, just about *half* of *all* deaths are caused by problems of the heart.

In the early 1960s, Dr. Christiaan Barnard, of South Africa, was spending most of his time trying to keep people from dying of heart problems. Dr. Barnard headed a team of doctors and nurses trained in heart surgery, and every day they did such things as repair holes in hearts and replace heart valves, giving scores of people a new chance at life. But, all too often, there were patients for whom nothing at all could be done—people whose hearts were so badly diseased that no repair was possible, and they faced certain death. Like other doctors, Christiaan Barnard knew that the only possible chance for such a person was to have the diseased heart *replaced* by a healthy new one. But this was something that had never been done and that some doctors thought could never be done.

The big problem about trying to replace a heart was what is known to doctors as "rejection." The human body usually just refuses to accept a new organ that didn't actually grow inside it and tries to reject the organ by literally attempting to kill it! However, Dr. Barnard felt that the technology of his time—the drugs, machines, and methods available to doctors—could prevent rejection. In 1962, he and some of the others on his surgical team began

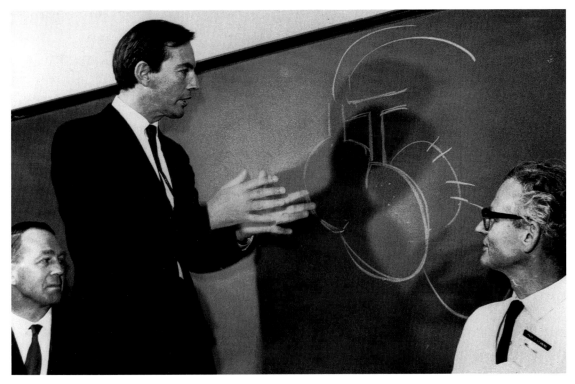

Dr. Christiaan Barnard speaks at a press conference in December 1967.

trying to replace the hearts of dogs and control the rejection that took place. By October of 1967, Barnard and his team had done forty-eight heart transplants on dogs, and Barnard felt it was time to try the operation on a human, to try to save a human life.

The patient chosen was a fifty-five-year-old man named Louis Washkansky, who was slowly dying of heart disease. His heart was enormously enlarged, his legs and liver were badly swollen, and he had frequent chest pains and great difficulty breathing. Doctors had no hope of his surviving much longer. When asked if he was willing to have this risky operation, one that had never been done before, he instantly said yes. For him, it meant a chance at life.

However, once the decision was made, Louis Washkansky lay in the hospital for three weeks, waiting for a heart to become available. Dr. Barnard became fearful that Washkansky would die before the attempt to save him could be made. Then, one night, Dr. Barnard received a phone call. A twenty-four-year-old woman named Denise Darvall had been hit by a car and badly injured. Her skull was shattered and her brain was so seriously damaged that it was literally dead. The woman was in a coma from which she would never awake, and her body was being kept alive only by means of machines. When Dr. Barnard asked the woman's father for permission to use her heart in an attempt to save Mr. Washkansky's life, the man agreed.

The operation took place on December 3, beginning at about midnight. Mr. Washkansky was brought into an operating room and put into a sleep with an anesthetic. The young woman whose heart he would receive was put in an operating room next door. Mr. Washkansky's chest was opened and his heart was exposed. Dr. Barnard and the others could clearly see how badly diseased it was—the left side of it was actually scarred. The team began hooking up the man to the machinery that would keep him alive while his heart was removed from his body.

Now the machine keeping the young woman's body alive was turned off. The doctors would not begin cutting into her until her heart actually stopped and she was fully dead. When this happened, one of the team surgeons removed her heart. It was connected to a machine that would keep it alive until it could be put into Mr. Washkansky's body.

The team of doctors and nurses worked through the night. At one point, there was a moment of horror when a mistake caused the heart-lung machine keeping Washkansky alive to stop working. Dr. Barnard later said that he feared the man was going to die before the operation could be finished. But one of the doctors managed to quickly fix the machine and the operation continued.

At the moment when Mr. Washkansky's heart was about to be removed, it went into a heart attack and began to beat irregularly. This would have killed the man at any other time, but now, working quickly, Dr. Barnard cut the heart free of the blood vessels holding it in place and removed it from Washkansky's body. Then began the task of putting the new heart in place, of making it start to beat by means of electric shock, and of closing up Mr. Washkansky's chest. By 6:24 in the morning, just about everything was finished. Mr. Washkansky lay sleeping, his fresh new heart beating steadily.

News of the operation caused a sensation throughout the world. For the first time in history, a human being's diseased heart had been taken out of his body and replaced with a healthy one. Sadly, even though Mr. Washkansky's new heart continued to work perfectly, he was only able to enjoy life for another eighteen days. An infection set into his lungs and he died on

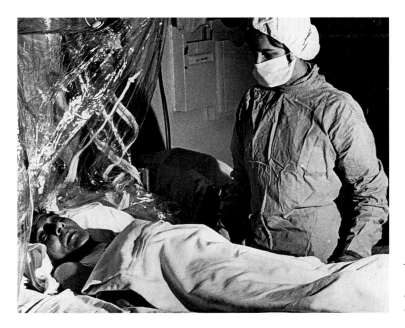

A nurse checks on Louis Washkansky following his historic heart transplant operation.

December 21. Nevertheless, the operation had been a success, and millions of people around the world were given new hope by it. Other doctors began doing heart transplant operations and such operations became more and more commonplace and successful. By the mid 1990s, about 86 percent of all the people who had had heart transplant operations in the United States were still alive and well a year afterward, and 65 percent had lived on for five years or more. Heart disease no longer automatically means death.

THE ARTIFICIAL HEART

For Dr. Christiaan Barnard, taking a diseased heart out of a person's body and replacing it with a healthy heart from someone else was the solution to a major medical problem. But some other doctors felt there was another approach that was better.

These doctors did not think that the use of another person's heart to replace a diseased heart was the best idea, simply because they felt there would never be enough "spare" hearts available. A heart used for replacement had to be removed instantly from the body of someone who had just died, and it had to be in perfect condition, but this was just not possible in most cases. Thus, many patients needing heart transplants generally had to wait for a new heart for a long time and might well die before a replacement heart could be found for them. What was needed, many doctors felt, were *artificial* hearts—machines that could do all the things a human heart can do. If such machines could be manufactured in large quantities, they would be plentiful and would be available the instant one was needed.

By the beginning of the 1960s, a number of doctors were trying to develop viable artificial hearts that could be put into a patient's chest to take over the work of his or her heart. But as the decade of the 1960s drew to a close, only one kind of artificial heart had been produced. Invented by Dr. Domingo Liotta and Dr. Michael DeBakey, of Houston, Texas, it was made mostly of silicone rubber.

On the fourth of April 1969, Dr. Denton Cooley, a heart surgeon at St. Luke's Episcopal Hospital, in Houston, began surgery on a patient with a serious heart problem. Dr. Cooley had intended merely to attempt some repair work on the patient's heart, but upon opening the man's chest, he found that the heart was in dreadful condition. Most of the muscle forming it had been destroyed and turned into a mass of scars. Repair was out of the question, and Dr. Cooley realized that the only hope for the man, Haskell Karp, was an instant heart transplant. But there was no human heart available.

Dr. Cooley knew of the artificial hearts that had been made by Liotta and DeBakey. None of them had ever actually been put into a human, but an artificial heart was the only chance for Mr. Karp. A quick phone call was made, and within minutes an artificial heart was at the hospital. Dr. Cooley put it into Karp's chest in place of his diseased heart.

The operation was a success. Soon afterward, Mr. Karp was awake and able to talk to the doctor. He was alive because inside his chest, connected to his living

Dr. Michael DeBakey, one of the pioneers in the development of an artificial heart

blood vessels, was a *machine* that did what a living heart could do! He was the first human being in history with an artificial heart.

Dr. Cooley had not intended to leave the artificial heart in Mr. Karp's chest permanently; the artificial hearts were not really perfected and there were risks. Karp had the silicone heart for only sixty-four hours. Then a human heart became available and Dr. Cooley replaced the artificial heart with it. (Tragically, Mr. Karp developed pneumonia and died some time later.)

The operation that took place on April 4, 1969, showed that a human being could live, for a time at least, with an artificial heart doing the work of a real heart. It was hoped that artificial hearts might

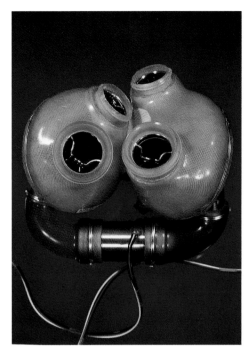

The Jarvik-7 artificial heart, one of several models developed during the 1970s and 1980s

become the best kind of replacement for people with diseased hearts, but no one given an artificial heart ever lived longer than about twenty months, and after a time they were no longer used. However, during the 1970s and 1980s, artificial hearts were used at times to keep people alive until a real heart could be found for them. Thus, they did play a role in helping to save some lives. And they helped spark an idea that was put to work in the mid-1990s— a number of people's lives were saved by means of a specially designed pump that is implanted in a person's abdomen and connected to the heart so that it can take over part of the heart's job. This shows great promise for the future.

5

SPACEFLIGHT

During the first forty years of the twentieth century, only a handful of scientists and engineers gave any thought to the possibility of space travel. Most everyone simply laughed at the idea.

But in 1944, when Germany was facing defeat in World War II, it unveiled a new secret weapon—gigantic flying bombs that were propelled by rocket engines. When these bombs, called V-2s, were fired off in Germany, they shot up into the air like skyrockets, reaching a height of 25 miles (40 kilometers) and following a curving path that brought them down to explode in England. Scientists everywhere realized that these weapons were actually primitive *spacecraft*! With only slightly more powerful engines, they would be able to keep on flying through the stratosphere and on out into space!

Immediately after the war ended, both the United States and the Soviet Union (Russia and the other Baltic republics, which then were all united under a single government) started work on programs to produce spacecraft. Using captured German V-2 rockets at first, and later building their own, they made higher and higher flights. Finally, in 1957, the Soviet Union launched a vessel that was able to escape from earth's gravity, flying into space and going into orbit around the planet. A little less than three months later, the United States launched a similar spacecraft. By 1961, the whole world was waiting for the first flight of human beings into space and the beginning of the exploration of the solar system.

FIRST INTO SPACE

On a flat desert valley in southeastern Russia, amid a cluster of square buildings, stood a gleaming object that towered several stories high. It looked like a giant metal cigar with a ring of cylinders encircling its lower half. Hidden

Yuri Gagarin awaits lift-off in the cabin of Vostok 1. *He would become the first man in space.*

from sight inside the object's tapered nose was a thick-walled hollow ball of metal, and within this, lying upon a padded chairlike couch amid a cluster of instruments, was a man. His body was covered by a bulky white pressure suit, and a round metal helmet with a glass faceplate completely encased his head.

The man was Major Yuri Alekseyevich Gagarin of the Soviet Air Force. The cigar-shaped tower in which he lay was the Soviet spacecraft *Vostok* (East) *1*.

After hours of final preparations, all was ready. Over the radio receiver built into his helmet, Gagarin listened to a countdown being made by a technician in one of the buildings: "—four—three—two—one—ignition!"

There was an explosion of flame and smoke from the cylinders encircling the spacecraft's bottom. As the energy from those twenty rocket engines thrust against the ground with enormous force, the vessel was pushed upward. Slowly, shudderingly, it lifted off the ground, seeming to hang motionless a short distance above the earth for a few moments. Then, as the thundering engines continued to push steadily against earth's gravity, *Vostok 1* began to rise, gaining speed. Trailing a long plume of smoke, it went rushing toward the stratosphere, quickly reaching a speed of nearly 5 miles (8 kilometers) a second. The continuous push against earth's gravity kept Gagarin pressed down into the couch as if a giant invisible hand were holding him firmly in place.

As the craft rose, bits of it were discarded. First, the tapered nose section was automatically opened up and separated from the craft, so that the metal ball containing Gagarin was uncovered. When the liquid fuel of the rocket engines was used up, they were also automatically separated from the craft, to fall spinning back toward earth. Finally, when a blast from the engine at the bottom of the long cigar shape supplied the final push needed to boost Gagarin's ball through the stratosphere and out into actual space, the metal cigar was also separated. All that remained were the metal ball and an attached squat metal cone that contained a small rocket engine.

Gagarin was now in orbit, circling earth in space at a height of more than 200 miles (320 kilometers), moving at a speed of 17,000 miles (27,200 kilometers) an hour. He made one full orbit, reaching the point above Russia where he had entered space in about eighty-nine minutes. There, he fired the rocket engine of the attached cone, which slowed down *Vostok 1* and pointed it toward earth. The cone now automatically separated, and only the ball was left, falling toward the earth at a speed of almost 300 miles (480 kilometers) a second. About 4 miles (6.4 kilometers) above the ground, a gigantic parachute opened up out of the top of the ball, and Gagarin floated gently and safely down.

April 12, 1961, was one of the most exciting and eventful days in the entire history of humankind. Yuri Gagarin became the first human to go into space. The great adventure of the exploration of space had begun!

Solving the Mysteries of Venus

At the beginning of the twentieth century, the planet Venus was generally known as earth's "sister." The two worlds are almost exactly the same size, they both have atmospheres, and their weight and gravity were known to be about the same, so it seemed as if they were much alike.

But Venus was actually a great mystery. It is wrapped in an extremely dense atmosphere, so thickly filled with clouds that it is impossible to tell, through telescopes, what the surface of the planet is like. Photographs taken through telescopes showed only a murky blur.

Astronomers could only make guesses, based on logic, about what Venus might be like. Earth's clouds are formed mainly of water vapor—water evaporated from the oceans, lakes, rivers, swamps, and forests—so astronomers felt that the clouds of Venus must be much the same. But the clouds of Venus are so much thicker than earth's that it was generally believed that Venus was probably covered with vast swamps and thick forests, much as earth was during the time of the dinosaurs. There was speculation over what kind of animal life might exist on Venus—something similar to dinosaurs, perhaps?

But later, better instruments showed that the clouds of Venus did not actually contain much water vapor at all. Astronomers were faced with the mystery of what they *were* formed of. To some, it seemed as if the "dry" clouds might be caused by enormous amounts of windblown sand and dust, and therefore the planet's surface must be mostly a gigantic sandy desert. Others thought the clouds might be formed of thick gases that boiled up from a vast ocean of *oil* that covered most of the surface!

When spaceflight became possible in the 1960s, scientists began to work out ways of using spacecraft to learn what Venus was really like. Both the United States and the Soviet Union began programs to launch "robot" probe vessels to acquire information about earth's "sister."

In 1962, the United States launched a spacecraft called *Mariner 2*, which passed within 22,000 miles (35,200 kilometers) of Venus. Special instruments for measuring temperature sent back the very surprising information that Venus was incredibly, sizzlingly hot, with a temperature that reached as high as 850°F (455°C). If a lump of lead were put down on the ground of Venus, it would instantly begin to melt! Obviously, no forests could survive in heat that would melt metal.

On October 18, 1967, the Soviet spacecraft *Venera* (Venus) *4* descended into the Venusian atmosphere. It somewhat resembled a winged insect body without legs, hanging from a large bowl. As it entered the atmosphere, a portion of it that was filled with instruments automatically separated from the rest and floated down to the surface beneath a parachute. This landing took about ninety minutes, during which *Venera*'s instruments sent information back to earth, revealing that the atmosphere of Venus was almost entirely carbon dioxide gas, with tiny amounts of water vapor and a few other gases. (On earth, carbon dioxide is a colorless, odorless, tasteless gas that is produced when anything containing carbon, such as plant or animal matter, is burned in some way.) Thus, the atmosphere of Venus was shown to be far, far different from that of earth.

The very next day, the American spacecraft *Mariner 5* passed Venus at a distance of about only 2,500 miles (4,000 kilometers) and detected another difference. Its instruments sent back the information that Venus, unlike earth, has almost no magnetism.

So, from 1962 to 1967, our knowledge of Venus was increased by a dramatic amount, and the idea of Venus as an earthlike world with forests and dinosaurs was completely destroyed. Today, with the knowledge gained in the 1960s and following decades, we know that earth's "sister world" is not much like our world at all. The surface of Venus is a vast, incredibly hot, rocky desert. In places, it is split by enormous chasms, one of which is 900 miles (1,440 kilometers) long, 175 miles (280 kilometers) wide, and 3 miles (4.8 kilometers) deep—far, far longer, wider, and deeper than earth's Grand Canyon. There are ranges of mountains and enormous volcanoes, which may erupt from time to time. The sky, with its thick carbon dioxide "air" and clouds formed mainly by droplets of searing sulfuric acid, is a sullen brownish orange in color, lit by frequent flashes of lightning and ripped by winds stronger than hurricanes. Venus is certainly a wonderfully interesting place, but it's not a bit like earth!

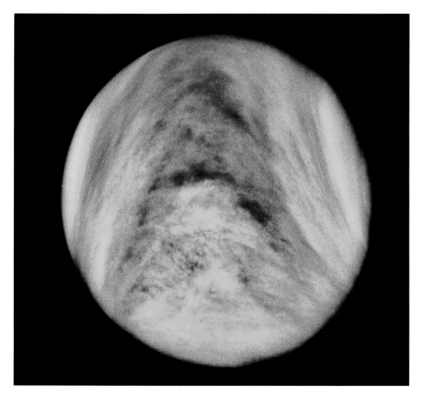

Study of the planet Venus continues to yield new information, even into the 1990s. This true-color image of the planet was returned by the spacecraft Magellan, *which orbited Venus in 1990.*

The planet Mars has always fascinated people. It is easy to see in the night sky because it shines with a distinct red gleam. Because of that, the ancient Romans gave it the name of Mars in honor of their bloody war god.

After the invention of telescopes, when astronomers could see Mars as a disk rather than merely a reddish speck, they noticed a number of grayish green patches on its red surface, and these became known as "seas." In 1877, the Italian astronomer Giovanni Schiaparelli thought he could make out lines running between the seas, and a number of scientists believed these might be canals, carrying water. Of course, this would mean that there were intelligent living creatures on Mars, for only intelligent beings could conceive and construct such things as canals.

The idea began to grow that Mars was an inhabited world, much like ours. In 1898, the British author H. G. Wells wrote a book called *The War of the Worlds*, about an invasion of earth by creatures from Mars. In 1938, a radio broadcast in the form of a play based on the book caused thousands of panic-stricken people to believe that earth really *had* been invaded by "men from Mars." Because of the excitement this caused, Mars became more "popular" than ever. Millions of people who didn't know the name of a single other planet knew of Mars.

Thus, with the beginning of spaceflight in the 1960s, there was tremendous interest in sending an information-gathering spacecraft to Mars. Now there was a chance to find out for sure if there really were intelligent beings living on the red planet.

The United States was first to successfully send a probe craft to Mars. It looked like an eight-sided metal box with four windmill vanes sticking out from its top. The vanes were solar panels that absorbed sunlight and converted it to electrical energy to run machinery inside the box. A bowl-shaped antenna, perched in the center of the vanes, was for sending television pictures back to earth. The craft was named *Mariner 4*.

Mariner 4 was launched on November 28, 1964. It reached Mars in the middle of July 1965, passing by the planet at a distance of 6,118 miles (9,788 kilometers). From that distance, it took twenty-two still pictures, which were transmitted back to earth.

The pictures were a total surprise. They showed that the surface of Mars looked very much like the surface of the moon. It was pocked and pitted with craters, caused by meteorites that had slammed into the planet over many millions of years. Mars has hardly any atmosphere, so none of the meteorites burned up as most do in earth's thick atmosphere; instead they hit the ground and left millions of craters.

No one had even suspected that Mars might look like the moon. Many people were disappointed that the pictures didn't show any canals or signs of life. However, it was pointed out that the pictures showed only a very tiny bit of the surface of Mars. It was clear that pictures of a much larger area were needed before any canals or signs of life might be visible.

So, in 1969, two more space probes—*Mariner 6* and *Mariner 7*—were sent to Mars, and these took 195 pictures from a distance of about only 2,000 miles (3,200 kilometers). They showed areas of dry red desert with rocky ridges and valleys, dotted here and there with meteorite craters. There was absolutely no sign of any canals, nor of any seas, nor of any living things. Mars appeared to be a cold, dry, desert world that could not support any kind of life except possibly microbes that might live in the soil.

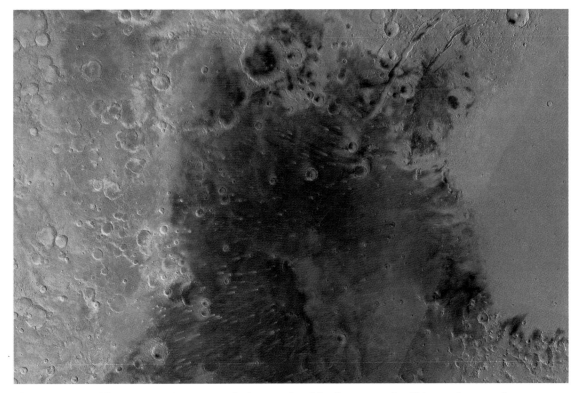

The surface of Mars is heavily cratered, the result of the impacts of millions of meteorites.

Thus, the U.S. spacecraft that flew past Mars in the 1960s put an end to the old idea of "men from Mars." But they introduced us to an interesting and awesome new world. We now know that Mars has huge volcanoes, mountain ranges, a gigantic canyon that's almost as long as the entire width of North America, and dry riverbeds where water once flowed. It is a place that will someday be visited by explorers from earth.

A "Walk" in Space

By the beginning of 1965, a number of men and one woman had made flights into space. There was no longer any doubt that the space age had truly begun.

But there were still many doubts and concerns about the ability of human beings to do certain things in space. For one, everyone involved with spaceflight knew that there would be times when something would go wrong with a spacecraft that could only be fixed by having a crew member go *outside* the vessel to make repairs. It was also the goal of both the American and Soviet space programs to construct a space station in orbit above the earth, and much of the work of constructing such a station would have to be done by people floating in space outside any vessel. But could human beings do such things? Some psychologists feared that a human floating in space with literally *nothing* around him or her might suffer mental problems, or even go insane! Doctors wondered if floating in space for a long period of time might cause problems for internal organs of a human body.

So, both the American and Russian space programs made plans for a major experiment to find out what would happen to a person who actually floated in space outside the safety of a space vehicle. The Russians were first to perform the experiment. On March 18, 1965, after months of training, Soviet cosmonaut Aleksei Arkhipovich Leonov became the first human being to take what the world's newspapers and television news reporters called a "space walk."

Leonov was launched into orbit in a two-person craft named *Voskhod* (Sunrise) *2*, piloted by cosmonaut Pavel Ivanovich Belyayev. When the craft went into orbit, Leonov began the experiment. Wearing a new kind of space suit that would protect him from the intense heat of sunlight, which is much hotter in airless space than on earth, Leonov went into a tiny compartment next to the craft's entrance. Sealing off the compartment from the rest of the craft, he opened the metal hatch of the entrance—a round opening just wide enough for a person to squeeze through. He put his head and shoulders through the opening into the blackness of space, then squirmed forward until he was completely outside the ship.

Leonov was fastened to the ship by a 16-foot (4.8-meter), tough, flexible metal rope. Pausing for just a moment, as if to prepare himself, he pushed away from the craft, floating forward until the rope was stretched to its full length. He was now in completely black, airless "nothingness," 16 feet (4.8 meters) away from the safety of *Voskhod 2*. He was spinning slowly at the end of the rope, so that one minute he looked up at the endless star-sparkling blackness of space, and the next he stared down at the earth, hundreds of miles below, looking like a vast modeled map.

This was the moment everyone had wondered about. What was happening to Leonov? How did he feel?

What Leonov later revealed was that he was sincerely *enjoying* himself at that moment! He found floating in space to be a very pleasant sensation, so much so that when he was supposed to return to the ship after ten minutes, he actually didn't want to! The American astronaut Edward White felt exactly the same way some ten weeks later when he took his space walk. "This is fun," White commented at one point, and when he had to return to his spacecraft, *Gemini 4*, he lamented, "It's the saddest moment of my life."

And so, the space walks

Edward White became the first American astronaut to leave his spacecraft while in orbit. He remained outside Gemini 4 *for a total of 21 minutes.*

of 1965 showed that human beings could work and perform tasks in perfect comfort, with no ill effects, while floating in space outside any craft. A major question had been answered, and a significant step in the advance of space-flight had been made.

HUMANITY'S GREATEST ADVENTURE

In July of the year 1969, one of the greatest achievements in the history of science took place. It was also the greatest adventure in human history.

On the sixteenth of July, three American astronauts—Michael Collins, Neil Armstrong, and Edwin "Buzz" Aldrin—stepped into a spacecraft that was designated *Apollo 11*. Their destination was earth's moon, Luna, some 240,000 miles (384,000 kilometers) away.

Preparation for this journey had actually begun years before. Very little was known about the moon when the decision was made to send an expedition there, and it had been necessary to find out as much as possible before the expedition could go. From 1961 to 1967, a number of unmanned space-craft had been sent to the moon, to take pictures and to determine if a landing could safely be made on the moon's surface. The kind of spacecraft that would carry the expedition and the kind of craft that would actually land on the moon had been thoroughly tested. In December of 1968, astronauts Frank Borman, James Lovell, and William Anders had flown *Apollo 8* to the moon, circled it, and returned to earth. In May of 1969, Thomas Stafford, John Young, and Eugene Cernan had flown to the moon and tested the landing craft, taking it down to a distance of 8 miles (12.8 kilometers) above the surface. Now two men of the *Apollo 11* crew would attempt to make an actual landing on Luna, becoming the first humans to set foot on another world!

As the long countdown to takeoff ended, the huge *Saturn* booster rocket carrying *Apollo 11* thundered up into a clear sunny sky. At the edge of earth's atmosphere, the *Saturn* was separated from *Apollo 11*, and a burst of energy from the *Apollo*'s own rocket engine thrust the craft on out into space, heading for the moon. The 240,000-mile (384,000-kilometer) journey took a little less than five full days, with *Apollo 11* reaching the moon and going into orbit around it on July 20.

Apollo 11 was actually formed of two vessels. The main one, designated *Columbia*, contained all the instruments, engines, and necessities for the voyage across space. Fastened to *Columbia* was a rather "buglike" contraption resembling a metal box on stilts, with vanes, disks, and square sheets of metal jutting up from its top. This was the landing craft, known as a lunar excursion module, which had been named *Eagle* and which would carry Neil Armstrong and Edwin Aldrin down to the moon's surface. Clad in space suits, the two men squeezed aboard—there was hardly enough room for both of them in the tiny craft—and made ready. Then *Eagle* was detached from *Columbia* and began the descent toward a broad, flat area that, centuries ago, was named the Sea of Tranquility (peacefulness).

There is no air on the moon, so *Eagle* could not fly down like an airplane, or glide down as space shuttles now do in earth's atmosphere, or even float down by parachute, for all these methods require air. It was actually *falling* straight toward the moon's surface at a speed of more than 2 miles (3.2 kilometers) a second! However, it had a powerful rocket engine built into its bottom, and by firing bursts of energy from the engine, Edwin Aldrin, the pilot, was able to slow the fall and guide the craft to a "soft" landing. But there were tremendous risks—if the fall could not be slowed enough, *Eagle* would *crash*, and if the ground where it landed was too rough, the craft could tip over and be damaged. Back on earth, the scientists and technicians who were part of the moon expedition program were awaiting the landing with their hearts in their mouths!

Then they heard Neil Armstrong's voice on *Eagle*'s radio: "Tranquility Base, here. The *Eagle* has landed."

The landing had been safely made. One of humanity's greatest dreams had come true. Human beings were on the moon!

There were television cameras mounted on *Eagle*, and many millions of people watching on earth saw what happened next. In his bulky space suit, Neil Armstrong emerged from the landing craft and made his way carefully down a short narrow ladder. At the bottom step, he reached his foot down gently to test the firmness of the ground, then put both feet solidly on the moon. "That's one small step for man, one giant leap for mankind," he remarked.

Neil Armstrong is now famous forever, of course, as the first human being ever to stand on another world. As the millions watched on television, Armstrong, later joined by Aldrin, tested the moon's gravity by running and jumping, set up scientific instruments with which they performed a number

Buzz Aldrin adjusts some of the scientific equipment that would be left behind on the moon by the Apollo 11 *crew. Note the footprints in the foreground.*

of experiments, and collected samples of moon rock to be taken back to earth for scientists to examine. The two men set up an American flag. On the windless, rainless moon, that flag, and the men's footprints in the dusty soil, can remain unchanged for millions of years!

After a time, Armstrong and Aldrin got back into *Eagle*, and a blast of energy from the rocket engine sent them speeding up to where *Columbia*,

HOW CAN YOU FLY WITHOUT AIR?

With no wings and a body built like a metal box with many corners, the *Eagle* couldn't have flown down to the moon's surface even if the moon had an atmosphere of air as the earth does. So, how was *Eagle* able to land on the moon without crashing?

It did so by using a fact of nature that physicists learned about long ago. That fact is simply that every action causes a reaction, or, in other words, every *forward* push causes a *backward* push. You can see this happen when you blow up a balloon and then let go of it. The air comes rushing out of the open end in one direction, and the balloon goes shooting off in the other. A push in one direction has resulted in a push in the other direction.

This is exactly how space vessels are able to fly in space, where a gasoline engine or jet engine won't work because there is no air. A blast of energy fired from a rocket engine in one direction pushes the craft in the other direction. And this is also how *Eagle* was able to land safely on the moon. As it fell toward the surface, pilot Aldrin fired quick bursts of energy from the rocket engine on the craft's underside. These blasts, pushing *downward* toward the moon's surface, had the effect of pushing the landing craft *upward*, which caused it to slow down. When *Eagle* was a short distance above the ground, Aldrin fired a long, steady blast that caused the ship to slow down enough so that it made a safe and gentle landing.

piloted by Collins, was circling in orbit. *Eagle* linked up with *Columbia*, Armstrong and Aldrin rejoined Collins, *Eagle* was detached in order to conserve on fuel, and *Columbia* started for home. The first manned moon expedition was a scientific and technological success in every way—truly one of the greatest scientific achievements in history!

Further Reading

Abels, Harriette S. *Stonehenge.* New York: Macmillan, 1987.

Baker, David. *Exploring Venus and Mercury.* Vero Beach, Fla.: Rourke, 1989.

Benton, Michael. *Deinonychus.* New York: Kingfisher, 1994.

Berger, Melvin. *Discovering Mars: The Amazing Story of the Red Planet.* New York: Scholastic, 1992.

Corrick, James A. *Mars.* New York: Franklin Watts, 1991.

Fraser, Mary A. *One Giant Leap.* New York: Holt, 1993.

Fromer, Julie. *Jane Goodall: Living with the Chimps.* New York: Twenty-First Century Books, 1992.

Gold, Susan D. *Countdown to the Moon.* New York: Macmillan, 1992.

Graham, Ian. *Lasers and Holograms.* New York: Franklin Watts, 1991.

Harlan, Judith. *Rachel Carson: Sounding the Alarm.* New York: Macmillan, 1989.

Lasky, Kathryn. *Surtsey: The Newest Place on Earth.* New York: Hyperion, 1992.

Miller, Russell. *Continents in Collision.* Alexandria, Va.: Time-Life, 1983.

Nardo, Don. *Lasers: Humanity's Magic Light.* San Diego: Lucent Books, 1990.

Reef, Catherine. *Rachel Carson: The Wonder of Nature.* New York: Twenty-First Century Books, 1992.

Roop, Peter, and Connie Roop. *Stonehenge: Opposing Viewpoints.* San Diego: Greenhaven, 1989.

Sullivan, George. *The Day We Walked on the Moon.* New York: Scholastic, 1990.

Vogt, Gregory. *Apollo and the Moon Landing.* Brookfield, Conn.: Millbrook Press, 1991.

Willis, Delta. *The Leakey Family: Leaders in the Search for Human Origins.* New York: Facts on File, 1992.

Yount, Lisa. *Pesticides.* San Diego: Lucent Books, 1994.

Index

References to illustrations are listed in *italic, **boldface*** type.

About the Author

Tom McGowen was born in Evanston, Illinois, reared in Chicago, and is a lifelong resident of the Chicago area. Married, he has four children and eleven grandchildren.

Mr. McGowen is the author of nearly fifty books for children and young adults, a body of work that includes both fiction (chiefly fantasy and science-fiction) and nonfiction. Two of his books have been named Outstanding Science Trade Books for Children; one has been selected as a Notable Children's Trade Book in the Field of Social Studies.

Mr. McGowen is a member of the Author's Guild, the Children's Reading Round Table, and the Society of Midland Authors.